Sadlier

We Believe™

Review & Resource Book

Project Director
Kathleen Hendricks

Contributing Writer
Cate M. Foley

Grade One

Sadlier
A Division of William H. Sadlier, Inc.

Welcome to the **Grade 1 *We Believe* Review & Resource Book.**

The activities in this book are designed to be used with the core chapters in the Grade 1 *We Believe* textbook. The activities connect to the "Remember," "Key Words," "Reflect & Pray," and "Our Catholic Life" features found on the *We Respond in Faith* pages of these chapters.

Included are questions that will help you remember what has been learned, ideas for prayer and reflection, and suggestions for living the faith in everyday life. Some activities are suggested to be completed with a parent or other family member.

For additional ideas, activities, and opportunities:

Visit Sadlier's

www.WEBELIEVEweb.com

William H. Sadlier, Inc.
9 Pine Street
New York, NY 10005-1002

ISBN: 0-8215-5421-2
23456789/07 06 05 04 03

Contents

CORE CHAPTERS

God Is Our Father

Remember

You are God's special creation. God has given you gifts. These gifts help you know and love God.

Work with someone from your family or class. Draw a line to match each flower to the correct sentence.

talk

learn

care

love

I can think and ______.

I can ______ for God's world.

I can share ______.

I can listen and ______ to God.

Key Words

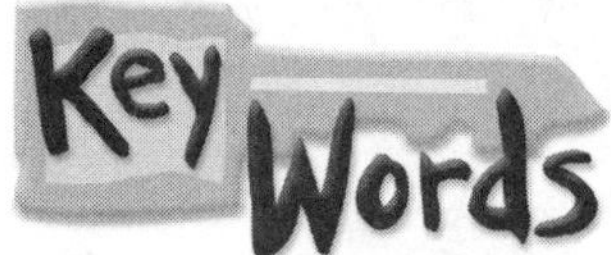

Creation
Bible

Read the clues in each space.
Use the correct **Key Word** to complete the sentence.

Draw a picture to tell about it.

______________________ is everything God made.

The ____________________ is the book of God's word.

Our Catholic Life

God wants people to take care of his gift of creation.

He wants us to take care of his world.

Circle the things you can do.

I can turn off the water.

I can plant trees and flowers.

I can pick up papers.

I can feed the birds and pets.

I can save newspapers and put them in a special place.

We Believe in the Blessed Trinity

Remember

We believe in the Blessed Trinity. The Blessed Trinity is one God in three Persons.

Write the names of the three Persons of the Blessed Trinity on the shamrock.

God the F__________

God the S__________

God the H__________ S__________

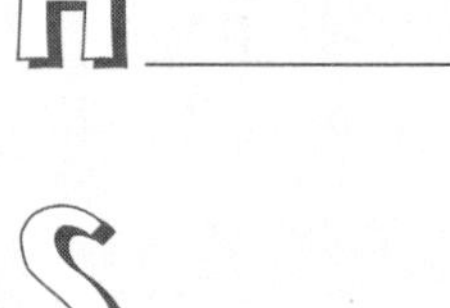

Sing this song to the tune of "This Old Man."

God the Father,
God the Son,
God the Holy Spirit,
Three in one,
This is the
Blessed Trinity,
Joined in love,
we do believe.

Reflect & Pray

God sent his own Son to us.
God sent Jesus to live with us on earth.
Jesus is the Son of God who became one of us.
Jesus tells us about God's love.

Write or draw a picture to finish the prayer.

Jesus, we

Our Catholic Life

At a special time, God sent his own Son to us.
Jesus showed us many things.
He showed us ways to show God our love.

Work with a family member.
Draw a ☺ if the sentence is a way we can show God our love.

- Read stories about Jesus. ◯
- Believe that Jesus is God's greatest gift. ◯
- Forget to pray. ◯
- Pray the Sign of the Cross. ◯
- Do not take care of God's gifts. ◯

Jesus Grew Up in a Family

Remember

Tell what happened. Put the sentences in 1, 2, 3, 4 order. Draw a picture to tell what happened next.

___ Mary and Joseph went to Bethlehem.

1 Mary and Joseph were waiting for Jesus to be born.

___ Mary and Joseph did not find a room to stay in.

___ Mary and Joseph rested in a place where animals were kept.

Key Words

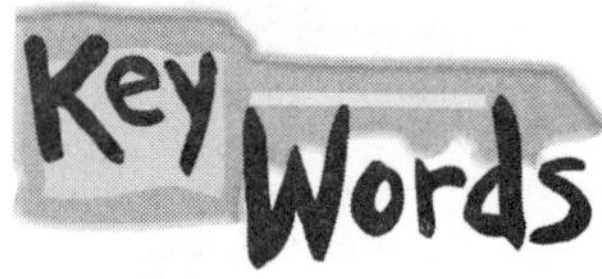

Color the word. Read the sentence.

CHRISTMAS

is the time when we celebrate the birth of God's Son, Jesus.

Write the names of the Holy Family near their pictures.

Jesus
Mary
Joseph

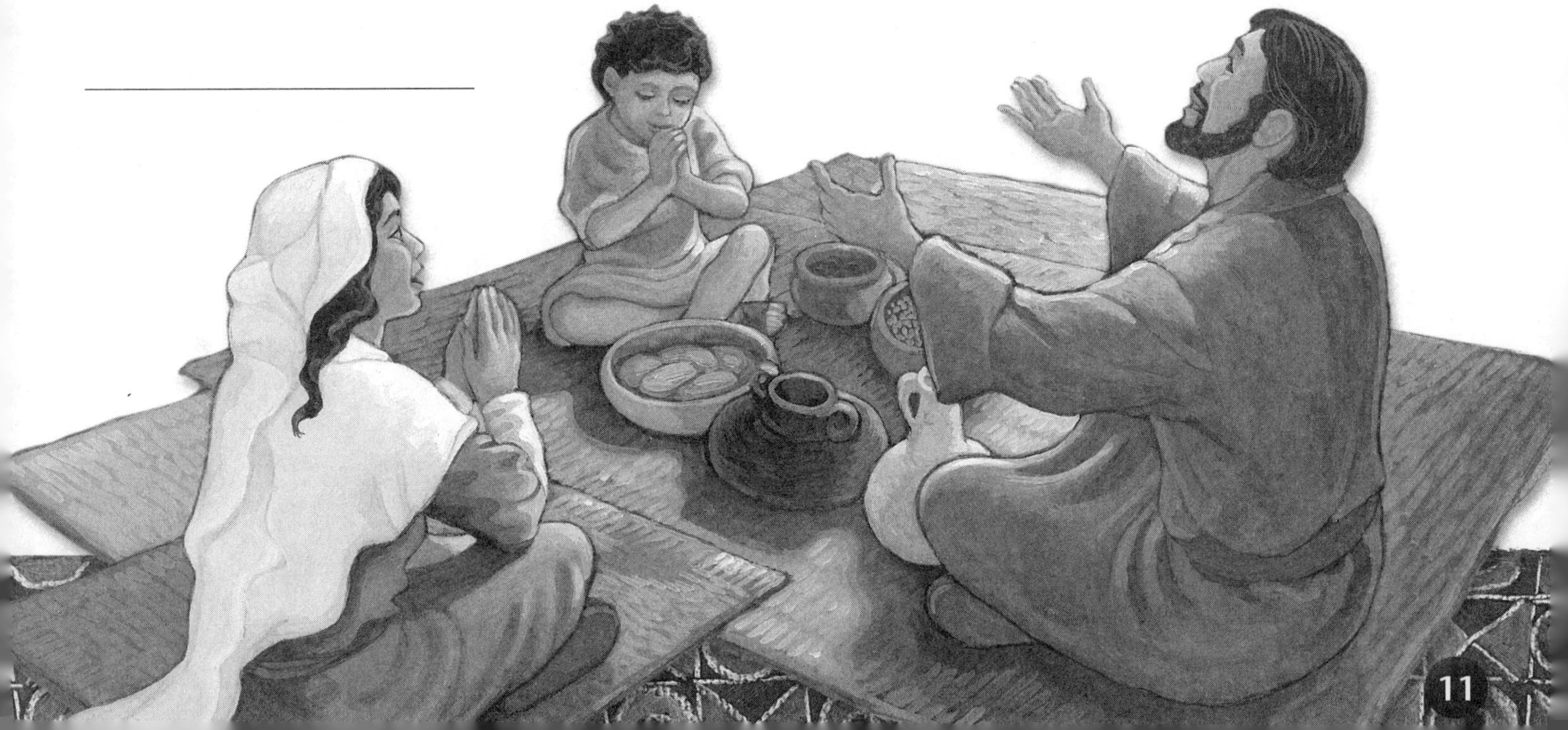

Our Catholic Life

Jesus lived in Nazareth with Mary and Joseph.
Jesus and his family loved one another.

Look at the picture.
Tell how Jesus, Mary, and Joseph are helping each other.

Tell how your family can be like the Holy Family.
Use the words in the box.

help	listen	pray	care

1. We can __________ for each other.

2. We can __________ each other in our homes.

3. We can __________ to stories about God and his people.

4. We can __________ to God together.

Jesus Works Among the People

Remember

Circle the correct words to tell the story of John the Baptist.

John was the (brother   cousin) of Jesus.

When John grew up, he became (one of God's helpers   a shepherd).

John told people to put God (first   second) in their lives.

He told them to share and be (selfish   fair).

People were getting ready to welcome (Jesus   Mary), the Son of God, into their lives.

Act out some ways you would get people ready to welcome Jesus.

Key Word

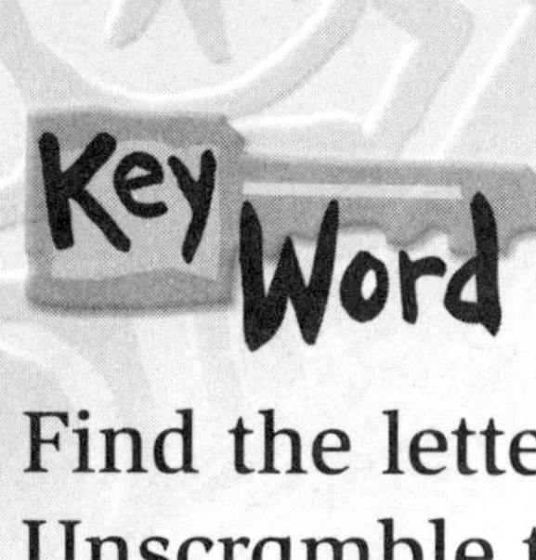

Find the letters hidden in the picture.
Unscramble the letters to spell a **Key Word**.
Write the word in the sentence.

When we believe someone loves us,

we ____ ____ ____ ____ ____ them.

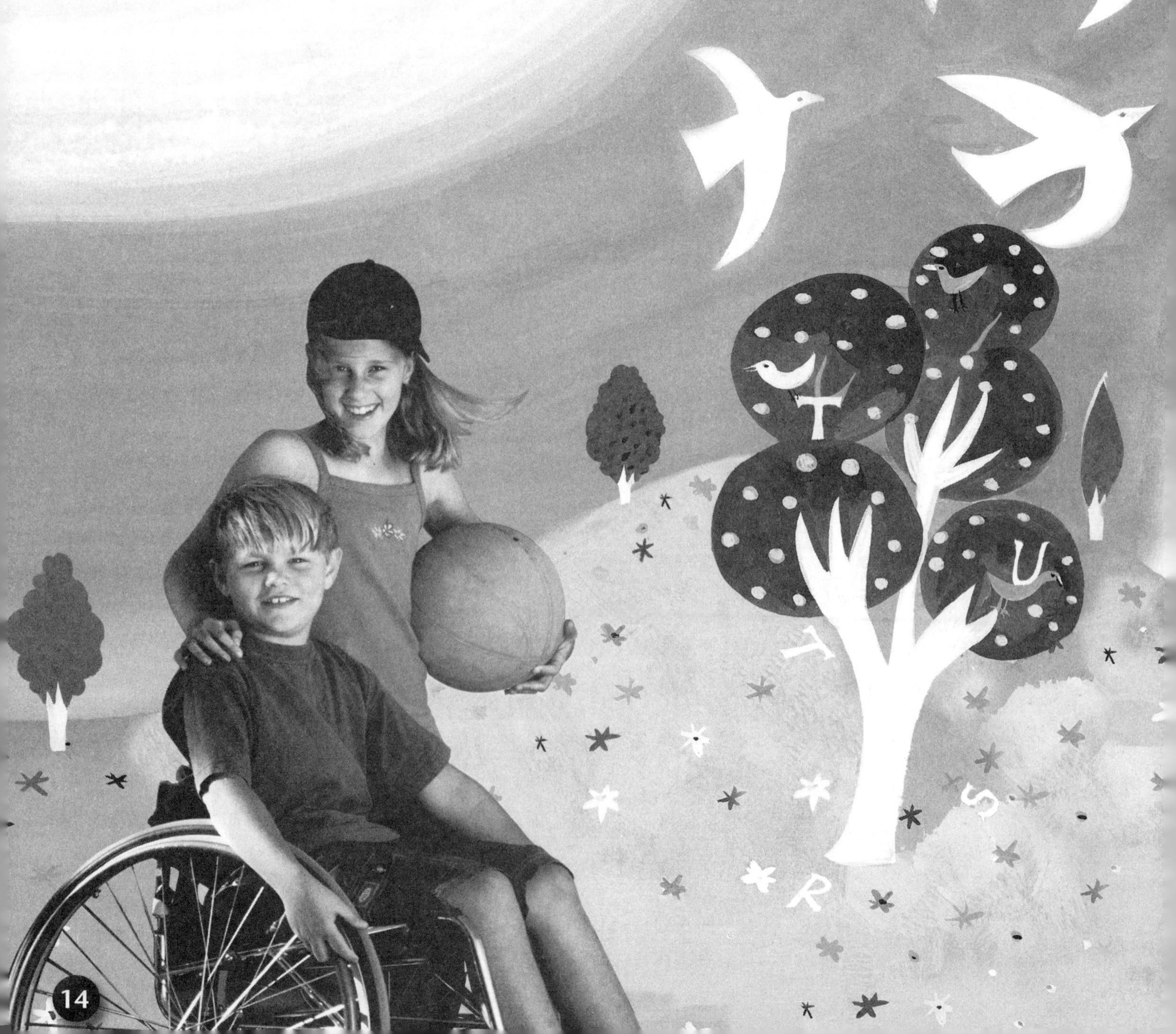

Our Catholic Life

Jesus helped all those in need.
He helped people who were poor and hungry.
He healed people who were sick.

Work with a partner. Make a card to send to someone in need. Plan what you will write and draw here.

Jesus Teaches Us About Love

Remember

Look at the picture. Draw yourself in the picture listening to Jesus. Share with your group what Jesus was teaching.

Reflect & Pray

Every week during Mass, we pray for people who need our prayers.

Talk with a family member or friend from your class.

Choose a person or group of people who are in need of prayers.

I would like to pray for

____

Talk about why you would like to pray for this person or group of people.

Our Catholic Life

Look at each picture.

Color in the ♡ if it shows how to live the Great Commandment.

Then draw another way to follow the Great Commandment.

Jesus Had Many Followers

Remember

Jesus invited people to be his followers. Jesus' followers learned from him.

Draw a picture of one of these stories. Then with a group act out the story.

- Jesus invites Peter and Andrew to be his followers.
- Jesus stops the storm at sea.
- Jesus shows his followers how to pray.

Find the missing words.

Cross out all the z s.

Write the words in the sentences.

The ___ ___ ___ ___ ___ ___ ___ ___ were twelve men Jesus chose to lead his followers.

z L z o z r d z s z P z r a z y z e z r

The ___ ___ ___ ___ ' ___ ___ ___ ___ ___ ___ ___ is the prayer Jesus taught his followers.

Our Catholic Life

Complete this activity with a family member or with a friend.

Read the first part of the Lord's Prayer.
Then place your right hand over the prayer.

Keep your hand there until you know most of the words of the first part.

Do the same thing for the prayer's second part.

Our Father, who art in heaven,
hallowed be thy name;
thy kingdom come;
thy will be done on earth as
 it is in heaven.

Give us this day our daily bread;
and forgive us our trespasses
as we forgive those who
 trespass against us;
and lead us not into temptation,
but deliver us from evil.
Amen.

Jesus Died and Rose to New Life

Remember

Draw yourself in the picture.
Talk with a family member.
Tell where you are.
Tell what is happening.
Tell what you see and hear.

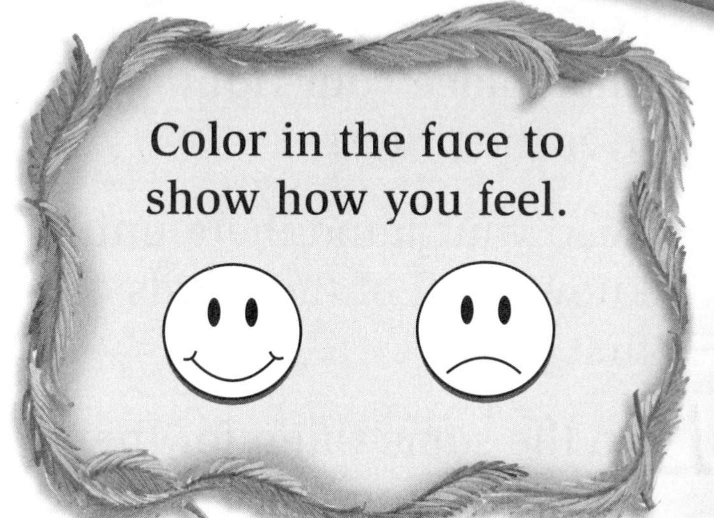

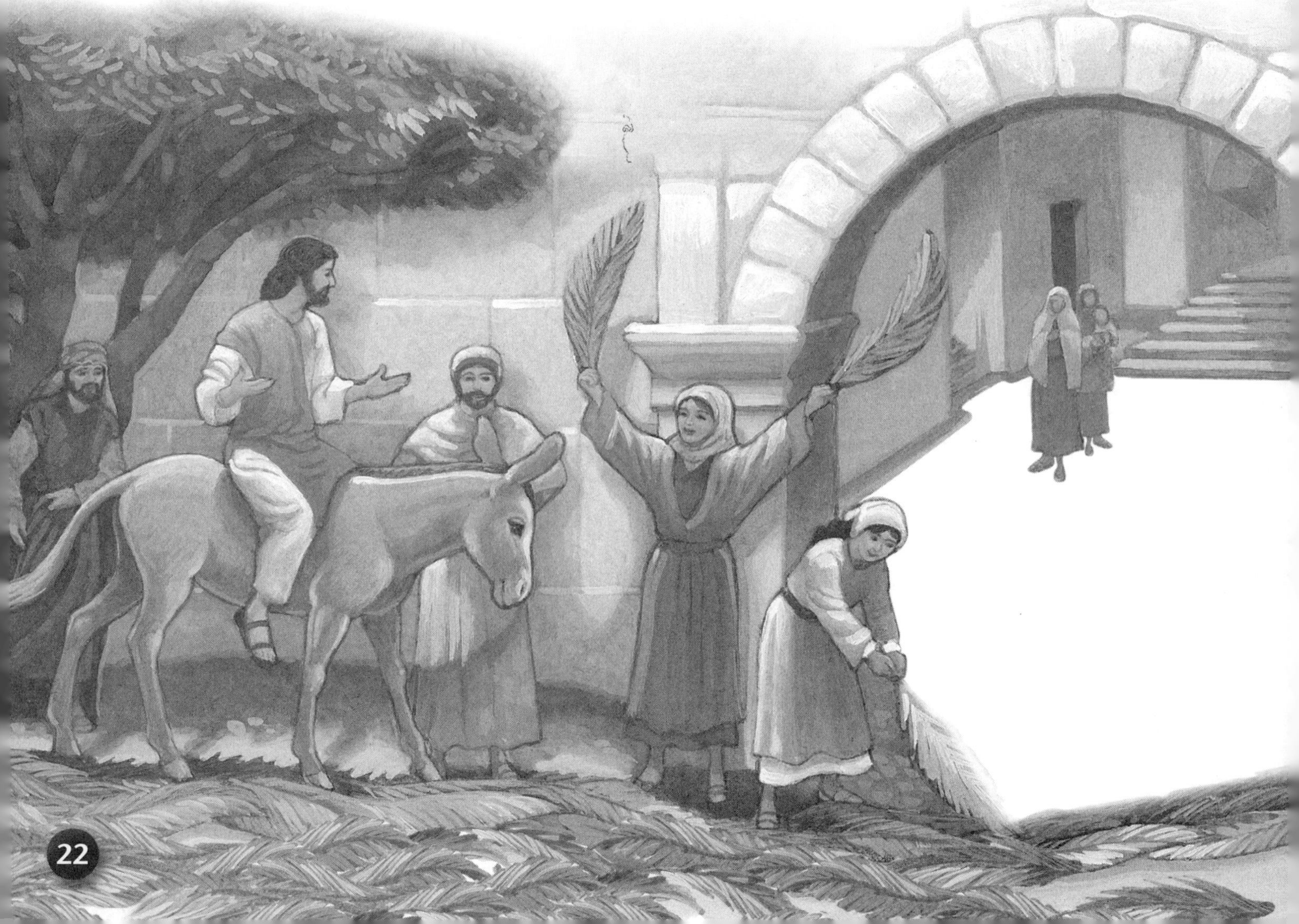

Reflect & Pray

Jesus died and rose to bring us new life.
Thank Jesus quietly.

Sing this song and do actions.
Then make up more words for the song.

Jesus Rose to New Life
(Here We Go 'Round the Mulberry Bush)

We clap our hands to celebrate,
to celebrate, to celebrate.
We clap our hands to celebrate
that Jesus rose to new life.

We swing our arms to celebrate,
to celebrate, to celebrate.
We swing our arms to celebrate
that Jesus rose to new life.

Our Catholic Life

Jesus is our Good Shepherd. He guides us, or helps us in many ways. Circle the ways Jesus, our Good Shepherd guides us.

Fight with our friends.

Share our things.

Be mean.

Listen to our parents or teachers.

Pray every day.

Jesus Sends the Holy Spirit

Remember

Use the words in the box to finish the story.

shore	nets	catch
breakfast	fishing	Jesus

Peter and his friends went

_______________________.

They did not _______________ any fish.

A person on the _______________
told them to put their nets in the water.

Their __________ became filled with fish.

The person on the shore was ____________.

Jesus asked them to have

_________________________ with him.

Find the word to finish the sentence.
Color all the x spaces.

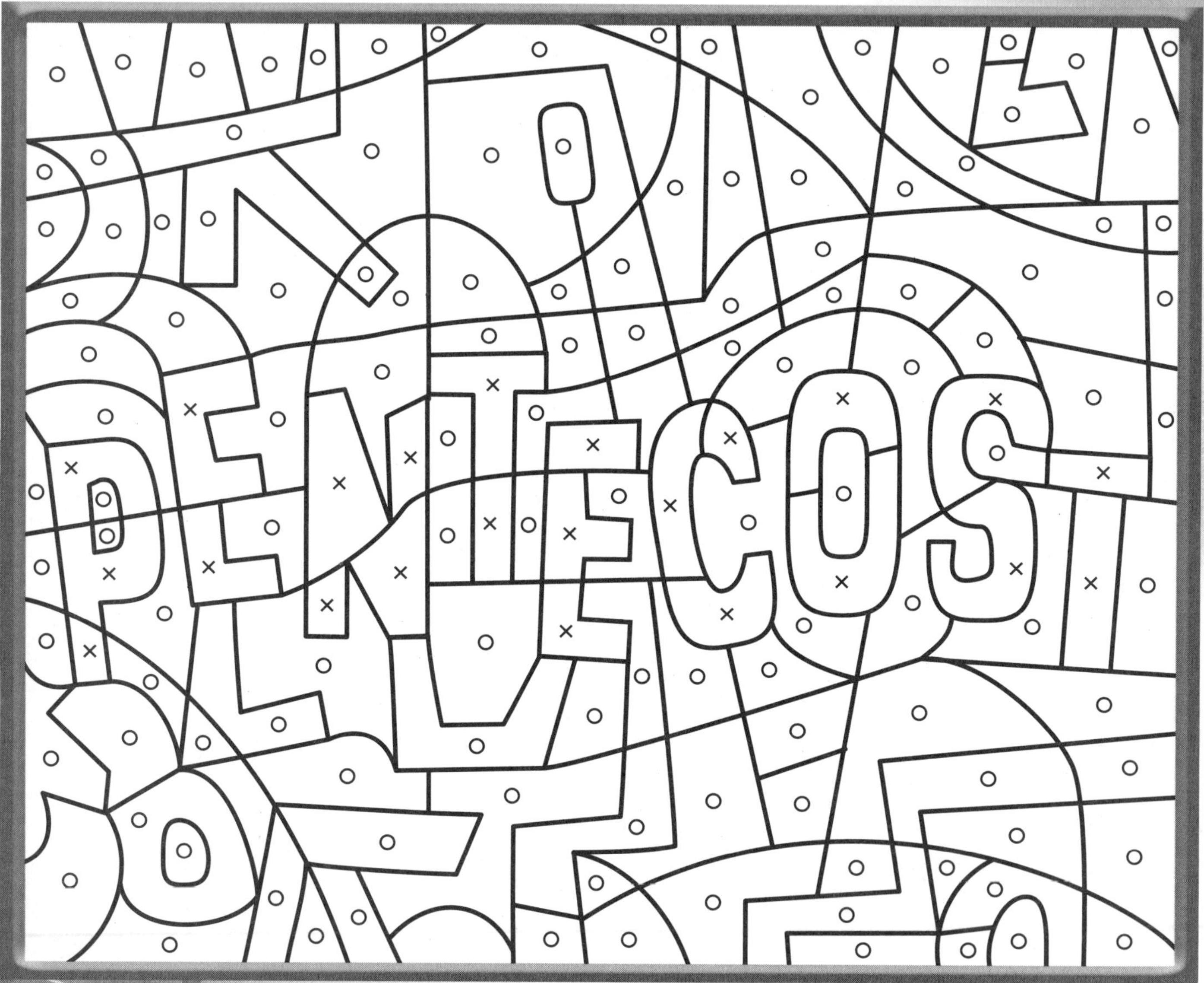

The day the Holy Spirit came to Jesus'

followers is ___ ___ ___ ___ ___ ___ ___ ___ ___ .

Our Catholic Life

Every day we remember that the Holy Spirit is with us.

Complete this activity with a family member or with a friend.
Draw a picture or write about the way the Holy Spirit can help you.

At home

With my friends

The Holy Spirit Helps the Church to Grow

Remember

The Holy Spirit came on Pentecost.
The Church began on that day.

Talk about Pentecost with
a family member or friend.
Tell who was there.
Tell what happened.
Would you like to have
been there?
Tell why or why not.

Act out what you would
have done.
Draw yourself to show how
you would have felt.

Look at the pictures.
Stand and act out what the Church is.

The Church is not just a building with a steeple.

The Church is all of the people who believe in Jesus and follow his teachings.

Think about some people you know who are members of the Church.

Write the first letters of their names in the flowers.

Our Catholic Life

The Holy Spirit is always with the Church. We can be like the first Church members.

Match.

The first members	We can
were kind and fair.	send cards to people in the hospital.
praised God.	share our food and snacks.
helped people who were sick.	be nice to our friends.
shared their things.	pray.

Write another way we can be like the first Church members.

____

____

The Church Serves

Remember

The apostles led and cared for the Church members. The bishops lead and care for their dioceses. The pope leads and cares for the whole Church.

Choose one of these Church leaders. Draw a picture to show how he serves.

Reflect & Pray

We serve others when we pray for them. Use your own words to pray to the Holy Spirit.

Holy Spirit, we believe you are with us all the time.

Holy Spirit, you are with the members of our family.

Help us to ________________________.

Holy Spirit, you are with the pope and the bishops.

Help them to ________________________.

Holy Spirit, you are with those who are poor and sick.

Help them to ________________________.

Holy Spirit, you are with those who are sad and lonely.

Help them to ________________________.

Our Catholic Life

Complete this activity with a family member or with a friend.

For each picture act out what you would do to serve. Then draw your own scene.

We Belong to a Parish

Remember

A parish is a group of Catholics who join together to share God's love. A parish is like a family.

Complete this activity with a member of your family or with a friend from your class.

Use the letters in the word PARISH to tell what people in parishes do together.

P ____________________

A ____________________

R ____________________

I ____________________

Sing songs to praise God.

H ____________________

Complete the sentences.

Find the answers by using the code.

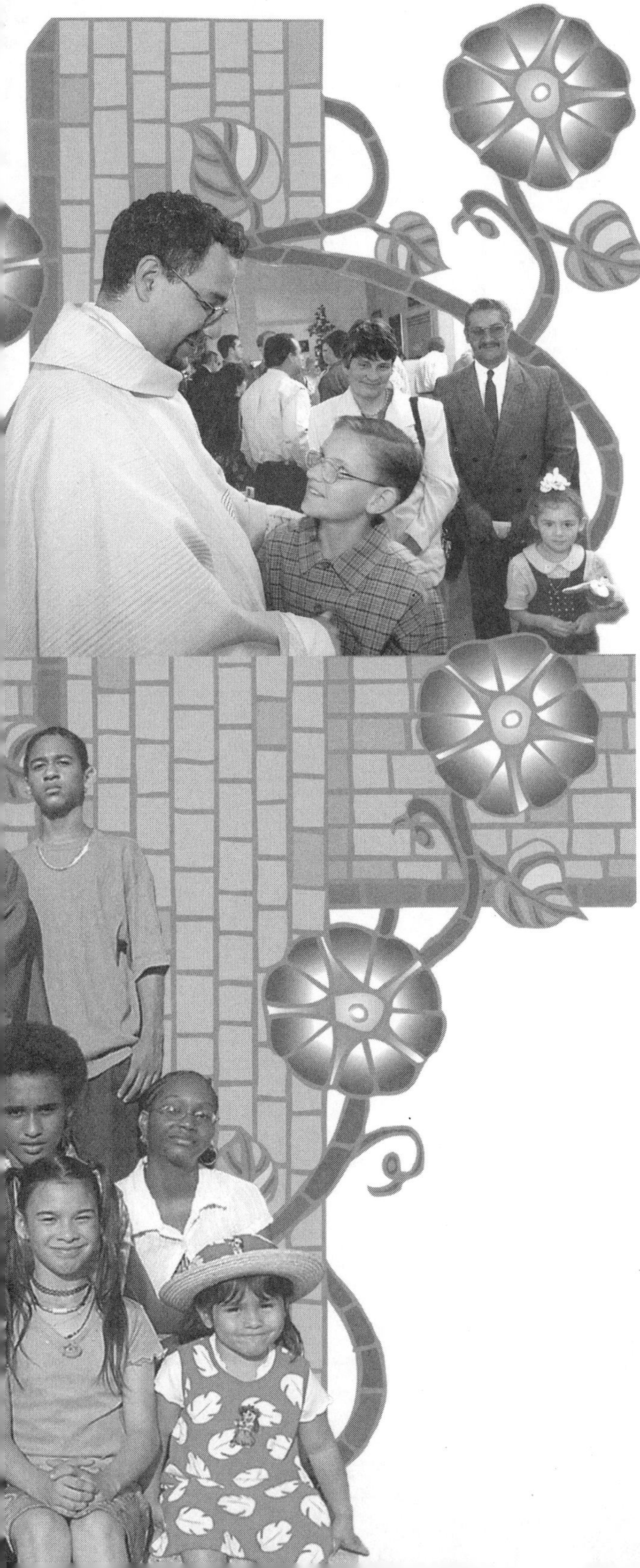

a	h	i	o	p	r	s	t	w
1	2	3	4	5	6	7	8	9

A ___ ___ ___ ___ ___ ___
5 1 6 3 7 2

is a group of Catholics who join together to share God's love.

We ___ ___ ___ ___ ___ ___ ___
9 4 6 7 2 3 5

when we give God thanks and praise.

The ___ ___ ___ ___ ___ ___
5 1 7 8 4 6

is the priest who is the leader of the parish.

Our Catholic Life

Our parish helps many people.
We gather food and clothes for those who are poor.
We send money to those who are in need.

Our parish cares for those who are sick.
We pray for them.

Draw a picture of how you can help others.

We Celebrate the Sacraments

CHAPTER 16
REVIEW & RESOURCE

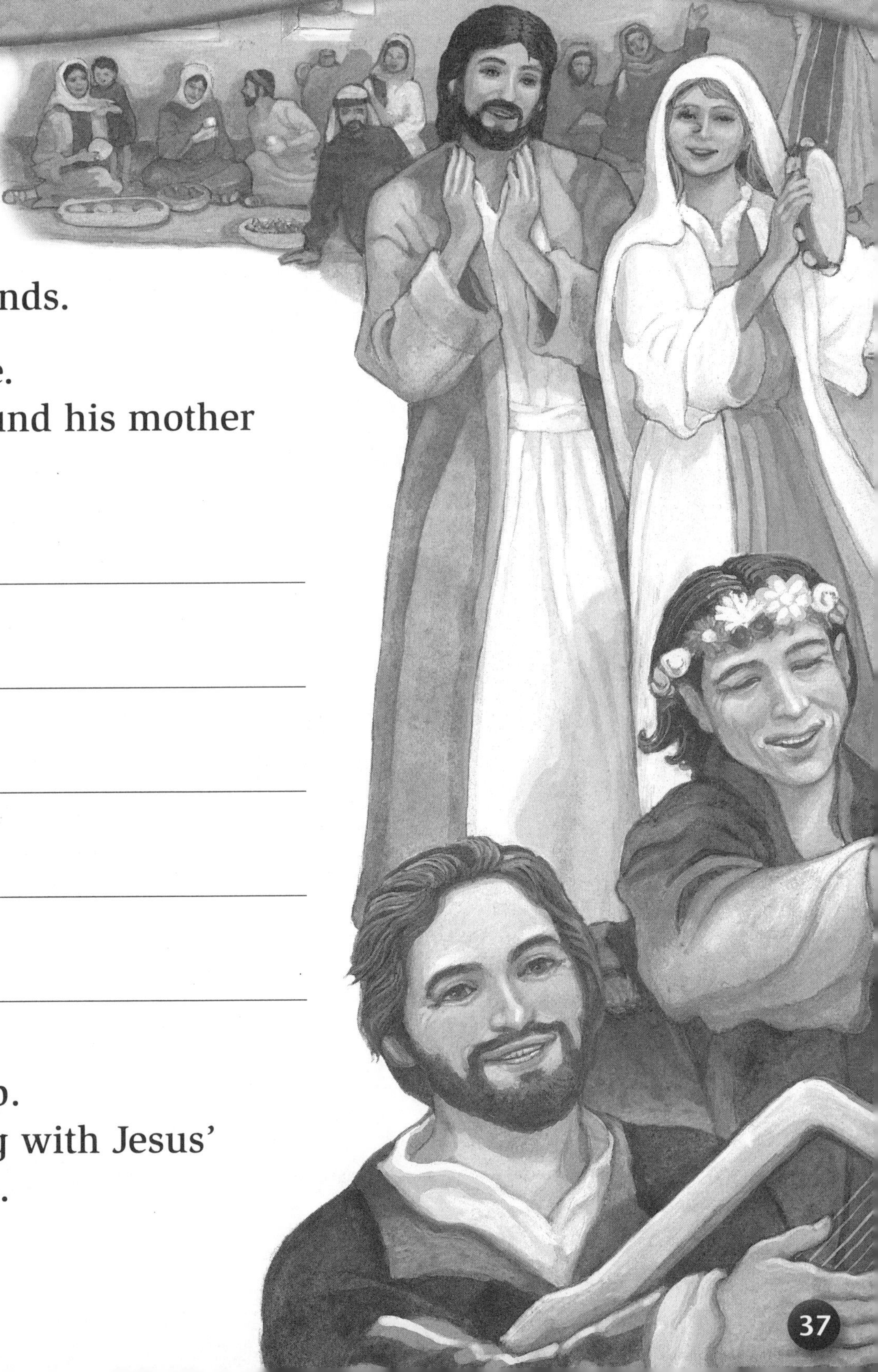

Remember

Jesus celebrated special times with his family and friends.

Look at the picture.
Write what Jesus and his mother are doing.

Work with a group.
Act out celebrating with Jesus' family and friends.

Jesus gathered with others to worship God. Together they prayed songs of praise.

Sing this song to praise God.

God, We Praise You

("Here We Go 'Round the Mulberry Bush")

God, we praise you. Alleluia,
Alleluia, alleluia!
God, we praise you. Alleluia!
God, we love—you.

God, we thank you. Alleluia,
Alleluia, alleluia!
God, we thank you. Alleluia!
God, we love—you.

God, we love you. Alleluia,
Alleluia, alleluia!
God, we love you. Alleluia!
God, we love—you.

Our Catholic Life

Jesus gave us seven special signs of God's life and love. The seven special signs Jesus gave us are called sacraments.

Complete this activity with a family member or a friend. Match each picture to the name of the sacrament being celebrated.

Baptism

Matrimony

Penance and Reconciliation

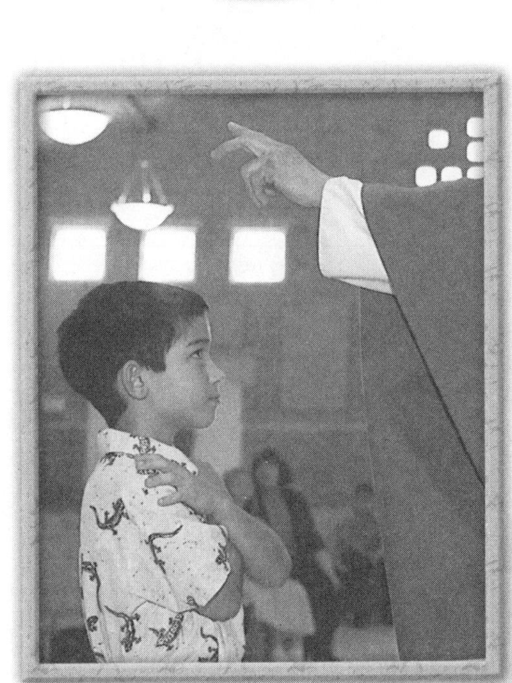

The Church Welcomes New Members

Remember

The Church celebrates Baptism with special words and actions.

Tell what happened at your Baptism. Put the sentences in 1, 2, 3, 4 order.

____ A candle was lit by my family.

____ Father poured water on my head three times.

____ Father traced the sign of the cross on my forehead.

____ A white garment was put on me.

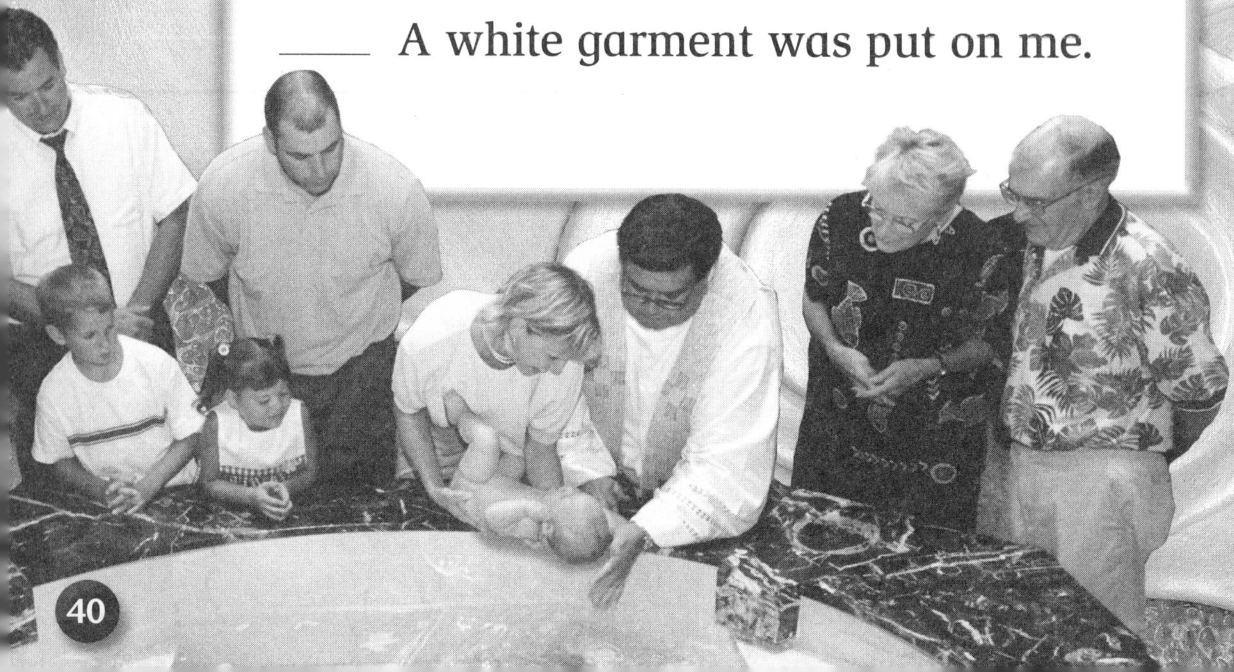

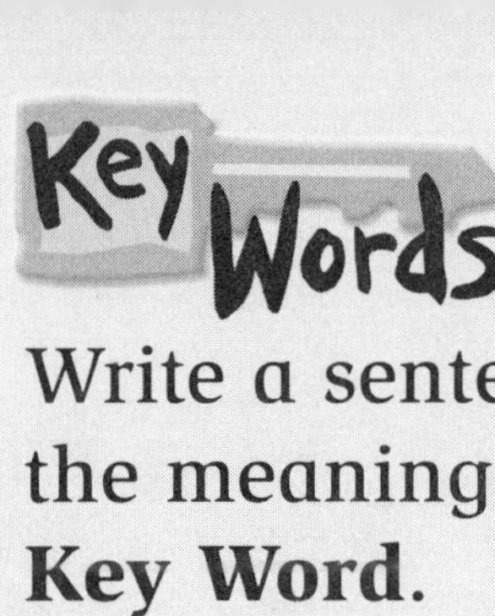

Write a sentence to tell the meaning of each **Key Word**.

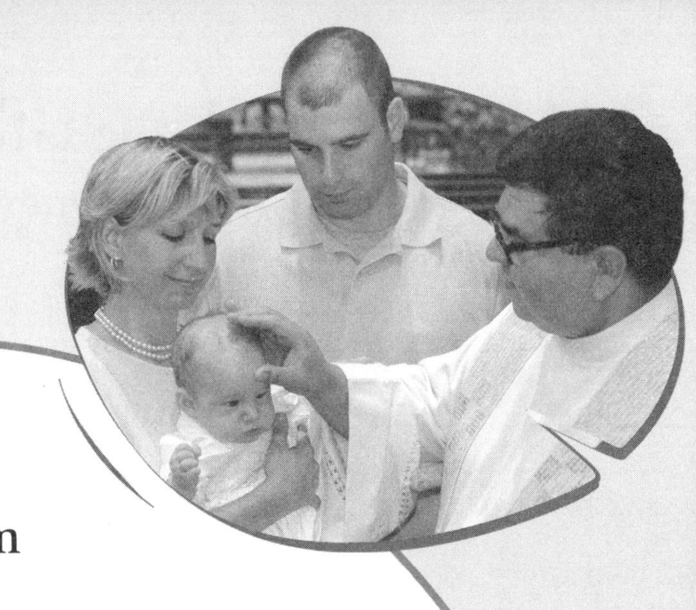

Baptism

grace

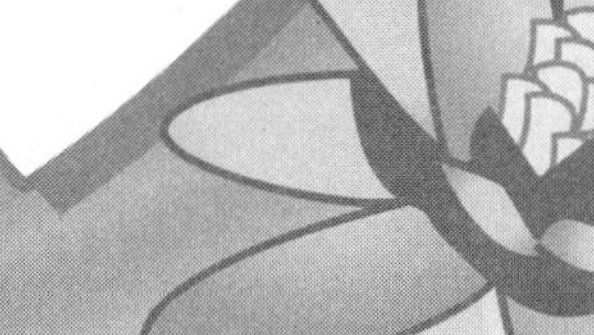

Our Catholic Life

You can welcome new members of the Church.

Complete this activity with a member of your family or with a friend from your class. Draw pictures to make a card, poster, or banner.

Welcome to

____

Parish Family

We Are Followers of Jesus

CHAPTER 18 REVIEW & RESOURCE

Remember

When we are baptized, we receive the light of Christ.

We are told to "walk always as children of the light."

Find the light of Jesus.

Color the path. Read the messages along the way. Act out doing one thing.

Reflect & Pray

Jesus wants us to get along with one another.

Jesus wants us to show love to others.

Jesus wants us to be at peace.

Draw a "picture of peace."

Then say a prayer that all people will be at peace.

Our Catholic Life

God asks us to choose to love him and others. He wants us to choose to do what Jesus taught us.

Look at the picture story. Color the candle next to the choice that shows how you can follow Jesus' light.

Your dad is raking leaves in your backyard. You choose to

jump in the leaves so he has to start all over.	put on a pair of gloves and help him.

We Celebrate God's Forgiveness

Remember

Complete this activity with a family member or with a friend.

Jesus told his followers that it is important to forgive others. He wants us to share God's peace.

Jesus told stories to teach us about God's love and forgiveness. One story Jesus told was about a loving father who had two sons. Tell the story in your own words.

Look at the picture. Write what you think they might be saying to each other.

Find the missing words.

Circle every other letter.

First word:

Second word:

h c i e j l k e l b m r n a o t p e

Reconciliation is the sacrament in which

we ______________________________

and ______________________________

God's forgiveness.

Our Catholic Life

Jesus wants us to forgive others.
Jesus wants us to share God's peace.

Look at the picture.
How can you share God's peace
with others?
Find the hidden ways.

Jesus Gives Us the Eucharist

Remember

On the night before Jesus died, he was with his followers in Jerusalem. They were celebrating a Jewish holiday with a special meal.

We call this last meal Jesus shared with his followers the **Last Supper**.

Draw a picture to show what happened at the Last Supper. Tell what Jesus did for us at this meal.

Reflect & Pray

At Mass we thank Jesus for all he has done for us.

Complete this activity with a family member or with a friend. Fill out these word cards to thank Jesus for being with us always.

When I am in my parish church, Jesus, I thank you for

____

____

____

When I am at home, Jesus, I thank you for

____

____

____

When I am outside, Jesus, I thank you for

____

____

____

When I am ______________,
Jesus, I thank you for

____

____

____

Our Catholic Life

Every Sunday we gather as a parish to celebrate the Eucharist. We take part in the celebration of the Mass.

Circle each way you take part in the Mass.

listen	**sing**	**yell**
stand	**sleep**	**pray**
play	**sit**	**kneel**

Write a story or draw a picture of how your family shares in the celebration of Mass.

We Celebrate the Mass

Remember

The Mass is the Church's greatest celebration.

Complete this activity with a family member or with a friend. Match the dots to complete these Mass prayers.

"The Lord be with you." ○	○ "Amen."
"Glory to God" ○	○ "in the highest"
"The Body of Christ." ○	○ "And also with you."

Put the words in correct order to complete this prayer.

ever God for be

The priest prepares the gifts of bread and wine.
We pray,

"Blessed ________________________________."

Key Words

We join together to celebrate the Eucharist.

Unscramble the words to complete the sentences.

r a l a t

The ______________________
is the table of the Lord where we celebrate the Eucharist.

e s l g o p

The ______________________
is the reading at Mass about Jesus Christ and his teachings.

Draw a picture for each Key Word.

Our Catholic Life

At the end of Mass, we are sent to live as Jesus' followers.

Look at the pictures. Draw a ☺ if it shows people living as Jesus' followers.

We Share God's Love

Remember

Jesus did what his Father asked him to do. Jesus told everyone about God. He shared God's love with all people.

Read the poem. Make up a tune or special beat. Make up actions, too. Share the poem with your friends and family.

Sharing God's Love

I can share God's love with you.
Jesus taught me what to do.
I can be fair.
I can forgive others.
I can share with my sisters
and brothers.
I can share God's love
wherever I go.
Closer to God I will try
to grow.

Reflect & Pray

Prayer is listening to and talking to God. We grow closer to God when we pray.

Here are some ways we can pray. Match each way with one of the pictures.

We can pray by ourselves.

We can pray with friends.

We can pray with our parish.

We can pray with our families.

Our Catholic Life

We love and serve God when we share his love with our families. Think about one way you do this.

Tell what you were thinking about. Draw a picture and write a sentence.

We Honor Mary and the Saints

Remember

God asked Mary to be the mother of his Son, Jesus. The Church honors Mary because she is the mother of Jesus. We honor Mary as the Mother of the Church.

Answer these riddles. Use the letters to find another name for Mary.

I'm in lap, not in tap. ___

I'm in cola, not in cold. ___

I'm in dawn, not in lawn. ___

I'm in yard, not in card. ___

We sometimes call Mary

OUR ___ ___ ___ ___.

How does your parish honor Mary?

Reflect & Pray

The Church has prayers to honor Mary. One special prayer is the Hail Mary.

Complete this activity with a family member or with a friend. Pray the Hail Mary.

Hail Mary, full of grace,
the Lord is with you!
Blessed are you among women,
and blessed is the fruit
of your womb, Jesus.
Holy Mary, Mother of God,
pray for us sinners,
now and at the hour
of our death.
Amen.

Practice the Hail Mary. When you can say this prayer by heart, color the picture of Mary.

Our Catholic Life

The saints tried to live the way Jesus asked. They loved God very much. They tried to share God's love with others. They prayed to God often.

Match the pictures of the saints to words that tell about them.

taught people in India

began schools for Native and African Americans

first priest in Korea

mother of Mary

Saint Katharine Drexel

Saint Andrew Kim Taegon

Saint Francis Xavier

Saint Anne

Act out what your favorite saint did to help others.

We Care for the Gifts of God's Creation

Remember

God has given us all of creation to use and enjoy. The world is full of beautiful places and wonderful plants and animals. God wants us to share these gifts of creation.

Write ways that you can take care of these gifts of God's creation.

Plants I can ________________________

____.

Animals I can ________________________

____.

Places I can ________________________

____.

Reflect & Pray

God has given us gifts and talents.

Draw or write about the gifts or talents God has given to you.

Thank you, God, for all you have given to me.

Our Catholic Life

Jesus taught us to care for and respect all people.

Complete this activity with a family member or with a friend. Read each story. Draw a ✔ by each way that you can show respect. Act out other ways to show respect.

A neighbor's beach ball rolled into your yard.

____ You say to yourself, "I found it. I can use it."

____ You give the ball back to your neighbor.

Your sister said something mean to you. She saw you were hurt. She said, "I'm sorry."

____ You forgive your sister.

____ You turn away from her.

Your little brother is afraid of a storm.

____ You call him a baby.

____ You sit with him and try to help him.

Vice President Publications, Sadlier
Rosemary K. Calicchio

Executive Director of Catechetics
Carole M. Eipers, D.Min.

Director of Research and Planning
Melissa D. Gibbons

Product Developer
Lee Hlavacek

Editorial Director
Blake Bergen

Supervising Editor
Mary Ann Trevaskiss

Senior Editor
Maureen Gallo

Vice President, Publishing Operations
Deborah Jones

Creative Director
Vince Gallo

Photo Editor
Jim Saylor

Acknowledgements
Excerpts from the English translation of *The Roman Missal* © 1973, International Committee on English in the Liturgy, Inc. (ICEL) All rights reserved.

English translation of the Lord's Prayer by the International Consultation on English Texts. (ICET)

Photo Credits
Cover Photography: Getty Images: *adobe church, chick.* Ken Karp: *children.* Jane Bernard: 35, 38, 53. Karen Callaway: 34–35, 39 *top,* 40, 41, 42, 52, 56 *upper center, center & bottom.* Corbis/Michael Pole: 14. Neal Farris: 6 *center right, center left & bottom left,* 7, 9, 19, 39 *bottom.* Getty Images: 6 *bottom left,* 44, 45, 63 *top.* Index Stock Imagery/Mark Gibson: 62. Ken Karp: 43, 45, 47, 48, 57, 60, 63 *center.* Greg Lord: 51, 55, 56 *top.* Masterfile/Allan Davey: 63 *bottom.* The Messenger/Liz Quirin: 39 *center.* SuperStock: 6 *top right.*

Illustrator Credits
Cover Design: Kevin Ghiglione. Teresa Berasi: 34, 35, 42. Joe Boddy: 18, 29 *kids,* 33, 45, 54. Janet Broxon: 4, 5. Chi Chung: 24, 46, 47. Christopher Corr: 13, 14, 15 *background.* Anna-Liisa Hakkarinen: 36 *bottom.* W. B. Johnston: 52. Jean Claude Lejeune: 32. Diana Magnuson: 8, 9, 11 *family,* 12, 15 *inset,* 16, 17, 21, 22, 25 *right side,* 30, 31, 37, 43, 58, 59 *bottom.* Cheryl Mendenhall: 25 *butterfly,* 26 *background,* 27, 61. Pam Rossi: 50–51 *background.* Molly K. Scanlon: 26 *line art,* 29 *flowers,* 50 *insets,* 59 *line art.* Stacey Schuett: 23 *frame,* 59 *frame.* Karen Stormer Brooks: 60. Matt Straub: 49, 51 *bottom.* Marina Thompson: 38, 39, 48. Amy Vangsgard: 40, 41 *background,* 62, 63. Carolyn Vibbert: 53 *top.* Sally Vitsky: 6, 36 *top,* 55. Mark Weber: 10, 11 *border,* 28.